Sally and the Big Slide

Story by Beverley Randell
Illustrations by Meredith Thomas

"Look at me, Mum,"
said Sally.
"I am on the little slide.
Here I come."

Sally looked at the big slide.
"I can not go
down the big slide,"
said Sally.

"Ella is on the big slide,"
said Sally.

"Mum," said Sally,

"I am going

on the big slide, too."

"Look at me," said Sally.

"I can see you," said Mum.

"Here I come!" shouted Sally.

"I am going down ...

down ...

down," said Sally.

"Mum," said Sally,

"I **can** go down the big slide."